M000011370

Sunlight

SUNLIGHT

Barbara Chung

CANYON WREN PRESS
SANTA MONICA, CALIFORNIA

Copyright © 2020 by Barbara Chung

All rights reserved. No part of this book may be used or performed without written consent from the author, if living, except for critical articles or reviews.

Canyon Wren Press
Santa Monica, California
www.canyonwrenpress.net

Cover design by Lluvia Arras
Cover and author photographs by Jack Smith

Sunlight / Barbara Chung – 1st edition
ISBN 978-1-7354489-0-9 (paperback) / ISBN 978-1-7354489-1-6 (eBook)
Library of Congress Control Number: 2020913948

For inquiries, email hello@canyonwrenpress.net

Printed in the United States of America

For my mother and father, and in memory of Ella

Contents

Weeping may endure for a night,
but joy comes in the morning.

—Psalm 30:5

Sunlight

Rain

When children walk in the rain, they look up,
tilt their heads back till grownups and houses
disappear, fill their vision with—with what?
I'll never know unless I look up too.

Cashmere clouds, gentle droplets that kiss
our faces, but only if we look through
the treetops, trace the leaves against the sky,
find haven amongst the loving clouds.

Trees, as wise as children, also look up,
reaching high to embrace the cloud-grey sky,
receive raindrop kisses to illumine
their leaves, kisses to set them verdantly
aglow, to draw forth their secret music,
songs glimmering green from rain-pattered leaves.

Breakfast

Sleep tiptoes away as the sky pales from
star-shot pitch to grey, preparing for dawn.
Bedroom doors creak open, slippered feet pad
to the kitchen in wordless alliance.
Coffee grounds purr as they pour, water runs
from tap to pot; the percolator hums
as it transfigures them into new life.

We awaken with the dawn, sipping slow.
We speak of our days' plans: work, shopping lists,
dressing cosily for the cold weather.
We warm pastries in the oven, butter
infusing the air, feeding us even
before we eat. O—this delicious
ether, these ordinary words, this peace.

Honeybee

O, you know how to eat!

Sometimes you zip lightly
from one open-faced poppy to another,
savoring a palette of delicate flavors
as a genteel gourmet.

Other times you roll decadently
within a rose's secret redolent depths,
an inebriate guzzling nectar,
unable to stand.

And you know how to save sweetness,
distill nectar to honey that will not spoil,
build storehouses to seal it with wax
against the hour of your need.

O teach me,
little one of translucent wings,
how to refine delight and rapture
that I may store them against the hour of my need.

Fatal Metalmark

Mourning Cloak, Funereal Duskywing—
I didn't know butterflies could be so goth
though I should have guessed
—they're famous for dying.

Well, not dying exactly,
but something akin,
larval body digesting itself into goo
within the pupal shroud.

Funereal Duskywing, Mourning Cloak,
Fatal Metalmark—
what else would you expect
with names like these?

Certainly not metamorphosis,
not transfiguration of post-larval ooze
into delicate wings, dancing flight,
the Fatal Metalmark's silvery gleam,
the Victorian lace of the Mourning Cloak,
the Funereal Duskywing's iridescent fire.

People who know such things say caterpillars
grow butterfly cells while still in the egg—

cells that survive chrysalid dissolution
to dapple the air with kaleidoscopic beauty.

I must remember this.

On the 7th of January, 2020

a woman checks the pouches of dead kangaroos
   for living joeys

sheep who once grazed in meadows now lie
   scorched and dead by the roadside

children shiver and freeze in the richest nation in
   the world, fingers burning from cold

war sears the mind of a mother's son as his legs are
   sacrificed to the vainglory of old men

quilters stitch mittens for burnt koalas, pouches
   and wraps for orphaned joeys and bats

women knit mittens to leave in a snowy park for
   blue-fingered children to take without shame
   (as if the shame is theirs)

sick in bed, fever-addled, i begin to knit a blanket
   for a baby due this spring

babies still come as we burn their world down

On the Last Day of May

sirens slice speedways through ocean air
for officers of the peace to teargas
those who peacefully offer their bodies
by the shore to shield those they don't know

under bluebird sky purple farewell-to-spring
and golden monkeyflowers grace
an oak-crowned slope with a painterly
backdrop for California everlasting

while people unmoved by everlasting
grace and unimpeded by conscience
or officers of the peace throw flash bangs
in neighborhoods where children and dogs play

ten years ago on the last day of May
a little golden dog in her first year of life
comes to her fourth home after the shelter
strangely wise knowing she would find peace here

helicopters hack night sky with drumfire blades,
searchlights searing our homes from on high
to tell us who is in charge in this country
indifferent to heavenly judgment

friends who knew the little golden dog
and friends who didn't, seeing sirens
flash bangs helicopters on the nightly news,
write to say stay safe shelter in place I love you

O the world can still be so beautiful

Here

"Why didn't I do better?"
"I should do better."
"I need to be better."

Hush, beloved.

We are lucky to have you here
—your breath, your eyes, your heart—
you, here with us.

It is hard to stand, to walk, to run
in ashen air, on jagged ground.

Yet here you are—
falling, bloodying your knees,
lying in the dirt,
struggling to catch your breath
—because you, O beautiful courageous one,
chose to stand, to walk, to run
in ashen air, on jagged ground.

Rest for a while, beloved.

We are in desperate need of beauty and courage.
We are lucky to have you here.

Listen

Do you ever wonder if you love too much,
feel too deeply, if you would be wiser
to guard yourself from injury and neglect?

I do. Sometimes I wonder like a plague.

Then I go into the woods, tell the trees,
whisper my secrets to the sylvan listeners.

With wisdom, the Tongva people called a leaf
and an ear by one word, *'anaanax*.

Sycamores know the hush that descends slow
and gentle as they drop autumnal leaves,
the return of birdsong with vernal birth.
Live oaks stand steadfast, listen evergreen,
withstand dissonance, await melodies.

Together these ancients counsel me.
They turn my confession into absolution.

I do not have their centuries to live.
I am but a murmur, then gone.
So I love tenderly, choose bravely,
fill my brief measure ere I run out of time.

Suicide Rock
(Idyllwild, California)

Life is terribly short and precious,
and I have important things to do:
caress the manzanita's lacquered bark,
savor the pine-spiced air, attend to the
tattoo of woodpeckers building their homes,
chill my bare feet blue in the mountain stream,
run up the trail with the deer, racing free,
chasing the sunrise to Suicide Rock.

My father taught me to find my own way
to these vistas; told me to stand up straight
on the steepest slope, discover safety
in what I fear. Now alone, I find newborn
strength abiding here. So I pursue life,
short and precious, in a place called Suicide Rock.

Embrace

(Hidden Beach, Carmel-by-the-Sea, California)

Turquoise waves catch the wind,
fling themselves white upon the rocks,
tumble me in fierce embrace
as they draw back into the sea.

O, to yield, to cast myself
after this wild tempestuous beauty,
to swim deep into the unfathomable—
but who can see the face of this mystery and live?

Sled Run
(Big Lake, Alaska)

Huskies made of soft fur and strong muscle
howl with impatient joy, flinging themselves
against the brake's grip, wild to pull our sled
over radiant stars and diamonds piled high
and soft under a cerulean sky.

I release the brake. In an instant—silence—
only pale swish of gliding sled runners,
happy breath of huskies born to this work,
strength flowing forward to carve wintry trails,
back through gangline to sled and into me.

Now I am muscle, joy, cold sharp breath,
boundless blue sky, snowy stars and diamonds.

Heaven must have winter, I think, dazzling
brilliance as dear as the most verdant spring.

Alchemy

The perfect chocolate chip cookie
(such a thing exists)—with crispy edges,
soft and buttery, elevated by
a few flecks of sea salt to transcendence
—is at a gas station in Los Angeles
just off Interstate 10.

Only in Los Angeles do you find
this peculiar alchemy—

all-American flavors of chocolate chip,
peanut butter, apple pie, recipes
composed as love letters for a new home
by a woman who fled a revolution,

bakers chatting up a Congolese customer
who speaks Lingala, Swahili, French,
as I translate with high school Spanish
my Korean parents thought I should learn,

as we laugh together and celebrate
the perfect chocolate chip cookie
in this bakery, in this gas station,
in this city, in this country that in
this moment is as golden as it could be.

Cinnamon

My mom told me cinnamon is good for my health
but I don't know the Korean word
and she didn't know the English one
so she said "that tree bark you like so much"

a perfect phrase to make me understand.
Once I dropped cinnamon donut crumbs
and my dog licked the floor for ten minutes
so she always got donuts after that

gazing at them to make me understand.
Once I found a small scar on her belly while
bathing her with cinnamon oatmeal shampoo,
worried over what made it, grieved that I'd missed it,

told my mom who said I understood her at last,
translated by that which speaks no language.

Christmastime

Holly garlands and holiday lights
deck the halls while monitor screens trace
vital signs in greenlit digits and lines,
hospitals always cold as December frost.

Yet Ella, always soft and warm, wearing
a badge proclaiming her a "volunteer,"
wags her tail as she walks toward a frail man
in a wheelchair and rests her head in his lap.

He and his wife begin to weep.
Hands with skin delicate as rice paper
bury deep together into golden fur,
receive grace from the gentle paw she offers.

On this night when a child was born in Bethlehem,
they mourn. Why? Only these three need know.

Waiting Rooms

They always look the same, the same square chairs
with wooden arms and legs, the same square-tiled
linoleum floors, scuffed but polished clean,
reflecting the same fluorescent lights above.

Nothing is the same, nothing, nothing.

Every time I wait in one of these rooms,
every time I sit in the familiar chair
on the familiar floor under the familiar light,

the one I love on the other side
of a door waiting in a body
newly unfamiliar in an unfamiliar bed

nothing else remains, nothing stays the same.

O, this love, this ache that obliterates
everything but this place where we wait.

Sentinels

Twenty-one days since I touched
someone I love.
The words have fled me.
I am bereft.

All the incandescent delight I once felt
cannot warm me now,
so ephemeral the assurance
of loving arms wrapped about me.

Potted plants sit by field hospital cots
surrounded by skyscrapers and sirens.
The small green sentinels stand guard
over frail bodies,
against the darkness encroaching upon
the void mercy left behind.

Silence

The quietest sounds fill this home with you:
a floorboard creaking under your light tread,
the quiet breath of your untroubled sleep.

You take one last breath as I say I love you.
Though I hold you close, your body grows cold.
Now the silence roars,
a thunderstorm shattering mountain peaks.

Rocks, soil, debris tumble within me,
howling wind tossing invisible wreckage.
I wake every morning on a pillow
storm-soaked by tears in my defenseless sleep.
My body defies gravity and stands
as I clutch the ragged edges of my heart
to hold this landslide of a soul within,
as I wait for mercy, for a still small voice.

Tonight

can i remember
when poppies became sunlight,
marine mist drew forth

essence of sagebrush,
sea and sky wrote each other
in bluebird sonnets?

Strain

my right middle finger, swollen, misshapen,
no longer mirrors my left

a physician would say i've torn a tendon
in the distal interphalangeal joint
i would say i've lost poetry
—those moments when my senses pierce my soul—

starved of broken bread and contrapuntal laughter
and gravity of another body on mine

still i write and write, trying to pierce my veins
with the tip of my pen,
draw blood to paint roses from words

but all i do is tear a tendon
in the distal interphalangeal joint
and even that pain is dull as the diagnosis

in this mist where only memory exists
i've forgotten to let grace breathe.

California Sagebrush

O my beloved, through no fault of yours
you set me weeping; just one breath and I mourn.
Sweet sharp scent that once tore me asunder
with delight, laying my soul bare and open
to the quietude of oak-clad mountains
and the winged whispers of butterflies,
to radiance of sun and warm salt sweat,
to birdsong, muscle ache, and rapture's touch,

you tear me asunder once again,
laying my soul bare to the memory
of what is already lost, sixty-two days
since jubilance, since I felt jubilance
of muscle ache, birdsong, salt sweat radiance,
and the breath of mountains dancing upon my skin.

Solstice

I love the winter solstice for being
the shortest, darkest day of the year,
for promising that every day after
will lengthen in beauty and light

even as its sister, the summer solstice,
ushers in the decline of days
when we slip inevitably away
from the sun deeper into darkness.

I would rather wait for sunlight than bid it farewell,
though the leavetaking be long and sweet.
What is more real? What we see today, or
what we become tomorrow, the next day?

I don't often tell people all this because
I don't know if I am being wise or naïve.
And always, the other solstice returns.

Birdsong

The air is delicious now,
clear as mountain water spilling
over this silent cityscape. I try

to savor it as I once savored sunlight
infusing my body like a seed
in dark tender embrace of rough soil,
quickening with breath of shared mirth,
encircled by shelter of muscle and sweat.
All in vain—air is not breath nor scent.

But wren and mourning dove delight
in the newfound beauty of their medium,
the redemption of their birthright.
Even at the gates of hell
they sing through the night
as if to seal the doors with sacred melody.

Like sunlight and soil, they owe me nothing
yet keep me alive.

Stillness

On days when honest labor of my hands
with earth and green things fills all my senses,
the sun stands still.

On nights when my soul skips and leaps alongside
words that tumble faster than my hand can write,
the moon stands still.

O—these moments when life is still—
quiet within the rhythm of my hands
as the light cascades over me.

Today

I will remember
when sun kissed newborn oak leaf,
raindrop tears fell sweet

and safe, sea and sky
ached for each other's embrace
as only they could.

Ladybug

Ladybug, why you won't leave my hand?
I hear you have connections in high places
—namesake of Our Lady of Sorrows—
and will bring me love, health, and abundance,

but you have more important
and more delicious work to do.

Here, let go my hand, step onto the narrow leaf
of this milkweed, tiptoe to its stem,
and make a lovely ladylike lunch
of that pestering aphid.

I thank you,
the milkweed thanks you,
the caterpillars and butterflies
who find their home here thank you.

As I marvel in a moment
I could never have imagined,
you bring me love, health, and abundance.

Heirlooms

In the cool of evening I sow the seeds (a gift)
damp dark peat and rough perlite (a gift)
between my fingers as I pack the pots (a gift)

tip from my bag every tiny rare hope
tuck each one carefully into its pot
cover tenderly with a quarter-inch of soil

arrange in the kitchen's greenhouse window

and watch them
and watch them
and watch them

and contemplate sleeping in the kitchen.

It seems a good idea I would later regret
so I go upstairs to bed and dream
of ancient spells disguised as small pale seeds,
enchanting from damp dark rough soil
glorious gleam of crimson and violet.

Seeds

I saw a first shoot shake off its loamy blanket,
stretch its first cotyledon, then its second
as I watched rapt for who knows how long,
mesmerized by the slender spine bent over

as it tugged on those two tender leaves,
pulling them free from the weight of sand
and silt and clay, lifting them up
to see the sun for the first time.

O seeds, tell me your secrets, you who know
how to safeguard your memory of sunlight
when darkness surrounds you, how to reach from
underground for air you have never breathed,

how to become the hidden ancient life
of mountains, unknowable and worth knowing.

Pandora's Box

The storytellers say Pandora,
seeing famine, war, disease escape her box,
had just enough presence of mind to slam
the lid shut before hope flew away too.

The storytellers say this means
that we hold onto hope amidst horror,
that hope remains fluttering inside the box.
Strange—why would we want to trap hope?

Still, the story gets one thing right—we humans,
we crush caterpillars and call them pests,
we cage songbirds and call them pets,
we claim people and call them ours.

Maybe that's our real sin and sorrow,
that we grab hold of what should be free.

Forgiveness

Every day, everything, everyone hurts.

But this is splendor. One wild purple sage sprawls
amidst carefully cloned yardscapes.

And this is festivity. Honeybees dance
with each other in rounds and waggles.

And this is richness. Salted butter melts
on warm bread, with a little strawberry jam.

And this is welcome. Hummingbird sage speaks
in the language of scent, "We're happy you're here!"

And I find forgiveness. For myself, for others.
What do we do when we must bear the unbearable?

We try, we fail—not always, but sometimes and often—
and we forgive. The world is too terrible

and too beautiful not to love each other.

Blossoms

Winds spin blossoms like snow from trees in spring,
whirling forth a petaled blizzard
under the clear blue firmament, while above

where Lyrid meteors fly with brilliance
unknown to sunlight, zephyrs kindle
the spark that starts a star seed, as under me

a seed's radicle forms within the husk,
cracks the shell, bodies its way forth into
the dark spinning earth in this universe

too vast and delicate to comprehend,
where life can glow with clarity, life will
blossom with snow-bright starlight in this

one irreplaceable span of breath.

Flame

I choose my own way to burn. —Sophie Scholl

Early in the morning I water seedlings
with leaves that look like poetry,
dance sprays of water over them
back and forth, back and forth.

The sun moves in the eastern sky
to catch the water's hand, sparks flying as
one starry rainbow dances after them,
back and forth, back and forth.

We dance together, sparks of water
and showers of light and one starry rainbow
and I, back and forth, back and forth,
till I leave, as I must, to return to the world.

When I leave, I carry these sparks within,
carry faith that we can dance with water and light,
flame forth in such beauty
that rainbows will chase us in delight.

In a world that denies fire and water,
that prizes dull embers and stagnant puddles,
calculated caution and cautious cruelty,
I choose my own way to burn.

Longevity

I don't always wish to live a long life,
but today I do.

I know longevity has its place
and I love my life dearly.
But sometimes I wonder if we must trade
between a full life and a long one,
between love and self-preservation,
and I know the choice I would make
though sometimes I grow weary
of choosing to love in a world that won't.

But today I went with friends to a barren valley
where we planted oaks and grasses,
mountain mahogany and sages,
watering the soil with hard work's sweat,
weaving laughter into the gentle breeze.
And at day's end, as we gazed at the valley
and imagined the woodland it would become,
I wished for a long life.

Willowherb

Unable to abandon slender leaves
and delicate pink and white petaled
quatrefoils to fade by the roadside,

I plant a half-dead willowherb in old soil.
Leaving it to wither would be worse still
than this quixotic attempt to save it.

It straightens its spine a little the next day.
Three days later, four green tendrils curl open
to reveal the spidery lace of white-fringed seeds

hidden within, each seed waiting its turn
to leave, to catch the wind and learn how to fly.
The world can still be so beautiful.

Treasures

I wish I knew how to write these poems for you.

When I was a child, I picked cherries from the cherry tree in the front yard with my mother, savored their sun-warmed flavor, marveled that my own hands picked them. Now, every time I eat cherries, I am the astonished child in my mother's arms.

Months ago, I knelt by a mountain creek and inhaled the morning fragrance of a small silvery sagebrush till I was drunk. Now I can summon the scent from memory, so piercing I taste it in my throat and fall dizzy once again.

Once upon a time, I had a golden dog so soft she knew that word—soft—so often did people gasp, murmur, sigh it as they caressed her. Now, though she is dead, I feel her softness under my hand as though she still lives.

～

Though I cannot find the words to help you taste, breathe, feel these treasures—I give you the person I am when I cherish small wonders, when I kneel before the unseen, when I remember love is stronger than the grave.

Speak, Love

You speak to me, low and gentle.
I glimpse my face, reflected
in the windowpane behind you.

O God—I didn't know
I could be this beautiful.
Speak, love. Set me aglow.

Canyon Wren

I love to hide, tuck my tiny ochre form
into cool crevices of rocky tumbles
and crags, small hermitages where I
prepare holy songs.

Then I soar high, sing till my body trembles,
send my wild white-throated canticle
cascading down in silver waterfalls,
summon enchanted echoes to the canyon,
awaken the dawn.

Hummingbirds

My mother's garden holds a hundred and fifty
rosebushes, riot of scent and color

matched only by the riot of hummingbirds
who streak the air with jewel-bright feathers,

finding camouflage here from predators,
from sharp-eyed kestrels, merlins, and hawks.

Beauty, only beauty, shelters beauty
from devastation. Isn't it always so?

California Avenue

The little girl who lived in the bungalow
on the corner of 24th and California
put a photo of my dog by her bed
"because Ella is my friend."

They are not here, but a western redbud
flutters blossoms and crimson heart-form leaves
in greeting, echoes the loving welcome
so often called out from the front porch.

Maria, who decorates her garden
near the corner of Chelsea and California
for Christmas, Easter, Día de los Muertos,
prayed for Ella every Sunday at Mass.

She is not here, but a coast live oak sapling
waves to me, showing off new leaves that shine
on a cloudy day and say to me,
remember us?

On the broad limbed companions of your childhood,
on the shoots forming from acorns you sowed,
on the ancient guardians of mountains
    where you kneel before mystery,
we are evergreen, evermore the same.

Dear friends, who wave hello and speak
happy memories to give hope of joy,
you are liveliest and loveliest
when rain draws near, when I need you most.

Sunlight (I & II)

Hopeful hands nestle an acorn's promise
of majesty in a pot of humble soil

the acorn slumbers, dreaming of the canyon
where its ancestors breathed before they fell

> She doesn't know what "cancer" means, only
> knows a visit to her friends in white coats

> helps her run for days after, dance in the grass
> wag her tail for joy, live with all her heart

Sleep slips away as the acorn extends
its first embryonic root to suckle

water and minerals, unfurls its first shoot
opens leaflets to sip sunlight greenly

> The size of her heart has doubled though she
> doesn't know it, doesn't know this tumor

> began in her mother's womb, only knows
> she loves her life and there's no time to slow down

We carry the seedling to the canyon
plant hope in its new everlasting home

tend it, water it, build it a shelter
from curious deer foraging for feed

> She knows this walk, knows our favorite walk
> the pond where she plays with children and ducks

but now—for the first time, she can't walk, though
she still tries, falling into tender arms

The youthful oak lifts new branches, future
home of birds and bulwark of animals—

stops short—trapped by the shelter now a cage
limbs spiraling, pressing against the walls

Let them go—now is the time—set them free

Let her rest in sunlight, in peace
sleep safe in unbroken embrace

Let it grow high where the falcons glide
keep the promise of its centuries

Acknowledgments

Writing seems a solitary act, but every piece I've written exists thanks to people who sought to make this world a better place. Many are friends and family who love me as the sun loves the earth, without reserve or thought of return, while others are strangers whose choices moved as starlight through time and space to illumine my journey.

I am grateful for the people who made these poems possible, who live in this broken world and yet believe we can make it beautiful. They remind me that it is enough to be kind and brave, not knowing the full reach of our lives.

Lluvia Arras, thank you for creating a book cover that faithfully reflects the poems within and for encouraging me to remain true to the calling. Jack Smith, thank you for chasing the vision of Tongva land that graces this cover and for so often lending me a space to dream and create.

I wrote *Sunlight* for my mother and father, who love me and whom I love, and in memory of Ella, who taught me how to be kind and live bravely.

Notes

Truth is more vivid than anything I can imagine. These readings sparked ideas and gifted me with a deeper understanding of their subjects and the poetry within.

≈

Albeck-Ripka, Livia. "Koala Mittens and Baby Bottles: Saving Australia's Animals After Fires." *The New York Times*, 7 Jan. 2020, www.nytimes.com/2020/01/07/world/australia/animals-wild-life-fires.html. Accessed 7 Jan. 2020.

Brock, Jim. *Butterflies of Southern California*. Pamphlet edition, Quick Reference Publishing, Inc., 2011.

Harris, Jenn. "What we're into: Cookies at a gas station in Cheviot Hills." *Los Angeles Times*, 30 Jan. 2019, www.latimes.com/food/la-fo-re-zooies-cookies-20190130-story.html. Accessed 9 Feb. 2020.

Jabr, Ferris. "How Does a Caterpillar Become a Butterfly?" *Scientific American*, 10 Aug. 2012, www.scientificamerican.com/article/caterpillar-butterfly-metamorphosis-explainer. Accessed 4 Feb. 2020.

King, Martin Luther, Jr. "I've Been to the Mountaintop." Delivered 3 Apr. 1968, Mason Temple (Church of God in Christ Headquarters), Memphis, TN. Speech.

@Sarah_Boxer (Sarah Boxer). "The seemingly miles of beds being set up at Javits. It is absolutely unreal to see what the National Guard & first responders have put together here in just days." *Twitter*, 27 Mar. 2020, 10:29 a.m., twitter.com/sarah_boxer/

status/1243591088411160576.

@stribrooks (Jennifer Brooks). "Downtown Minneapolis park benches are covered with brand-new hats, gloves, blankets and boots for anyone who needs them." *Twitter*, 6 Jan. 2020, 5:28 p.m., twitter.com/stribrooks/status/1214358228915671041.

Tongva Language. Tongva word of the day—'anaanax "its leaf." *Facebook*, 29 Jan. 2020, 11:30 a.m., www.facebook.com/TongvaLanguage/posts/2657372734380504. Accessed 29 Jan. 2020.

Wilson, Cintra. "You Just Can't Kill It." *The New York Times*, 17 Sept. 2008, www.nytimes.com/2008/09/18/fashion/18GOTH.html. Accessed 4 Feb. 2020.

About the Author

Barbara Chung studied at Harvard University and University of California, Los Angeles, and works as a strategic advisor to food and beverage companies. She lives in Santa Monica, California.